A Guide for Using

The Polar Express

in the Classroom

Based on the book written by Chris Van Allsburg

This guide written by Susan Kilpatrick

Teacher Created Materials, Inc.
6421 Industry Way
Westminster, CA 92683
www.teachercreated.com
©1995 Teacher Created Materials, Inc.
Reprinted, 2004
Made in U.S.A.
ISBN-1-55734-543-0

Illustrated by
Barbara Lorseyedi

Edited by
Candyce Norvell

Cover Art by
Wendy Chang

Table of Contents

Introduction and Sample Lessons

A good book can touch the lives of children like a good friend. Great care has been taken in selecting the books and activities featured in the *Literature Units* series. Teachers who use the activities here to supplement their own ideas can follow one of the following methods.

A Sample Lesson Plan

Each of the lessons suggested below can take from one to several days to complete and can include all or some of the suggested activities.

A Unit Planner

If you wish to tailor the suggestions on pages 6–11 in a format other than that prescribed below, use the "Unit Planner" on page 4. For any specific day, you may choose the activities you wish to include by writing the activity number or a brief notation about the lesson in the "Unit Activities" section. Space has also been provided for other related notes and comments. Reproduce copies of page 4 as needed.

Sample Lesson Plan

Lesson 1

- Prepare the "Pocket Chart Activities" (pages 12–13).
- Set the stage by completing a winter holidays unit (activity 2, page 6).
- Read "About the Author" (page 5).
- Discuss the new vocabulary (page 6).
- Prepare to read by completing activities 3, 4, 5, 6, and 7 in the "Before the Book" Section on pages 6–7.
- Read the book for enjoyment.

Lesson 2

- Read the story a second time.
- Prepare pocket chart and use the Bloom's Taxonomy cards and activities to involve students in critical thinking (pages 12–15).
- Use the sentence strips on page 16.
- Recite "The Silver Bell" (page 17).
- Create "Found Poetry" about *The Polar Express* (page 27).

Lesson 3

- Have children construct and write in "Polar Express Scrapbooks" (page 22).
- Complete the winter graphing activity (page 41).
- Practice alphabetizing with "ABC Harness Bells" (page 24).
- Begin practicing the Reader's Theater script (pages 45–47).

Lesson 4

- Complete "Simile Stars" and add to artwork (page 26).
- Learn a song about *The Polar Express* (page 42).
- Complete the "Bells Are Ringing!" writing (page 28).
- Practice the Reader's Theater script (pages 45–47).

Lesson 5

- Create "Holiday Banners" to give as gifts (page 43).
- Learn about sound with "Ring Those Bells" activity (page 40).
- Practice the Reader's Theater script, poem, and song (pages 45–47).

Lesson 6

- Discuss and write about the true spirit of Christmas. Display on a class holly wreath chart (page 30).
- Make candy houses (page 32).
- Follow directions to complete a picture (page 29).
- Create holiday ornaments to use in the Reader's Theater presentation (page 25).
- Prepare food to serve after the Reader's Theater presentation (page 31).
- Present "The Spirit of Christmas" as a culminating activity. (See page 44 for suggestions).

Unit Planner

Unit Activities

Date:

Notes/Comments

Unit Activities

Date:

Notes/Comments

Unit Activities

Date:

Notes/Comments

Unit Activities

Date:

Notes/Comments

Unit Activities

Date:

Notes/Comments

Unit Activities

Date:

Notes/Comments

4

Getting to Know the Book and Author

(The Polar Express is published in the U.S. by Houghton Mifflin, 1985. It is also available in Canada from Thomas Allen & Son, In U.K. from Cassell, and in Australia from Jackaranda Wiley.)

About the Book

Late one Christmas Eve as everyone is sleeping, a young boy hears a strange noise in front of his house. Tiptoeing outside, he discovers a mysterious train and boards the Polar Express bound for the North Pole.

Upon arrival in North Pole City, the boy meets Santa, who chooses him to receive the first gift of the Christmas season. Modestly, he asks for one silver bell from the harness of a reindeer.

After he boards the train for the trip home, the boy discovers to his dismay that he has lost the bell. On Christmas morning, however, he finds a small package from Santa under the tree. When he opens it, he is delighted to see that it contains his bell.

The boy and his sister marvel at the bell's beautiful ring, but their parents cannot hear a thing and think it is broken. For you see, only those who believe can hear the sound of the bell.

About the Author

Chris Van Allsburg was born in Grand Rapids, Michigan, in 1949. He graduated from the University of Michigan and the Rhode Island School of Design. Although his original dream was to be an artist/sculptor, Chris Van Allsburg was urged by his wife, an elementary school teacher, to use his talents as an illustrator of children's stories.

Chris was once asked where his creative ideas come from. His reply was, "They are beamed to me from outer space." Although he was joking, Mr. Van Allsburg's point was that he does not know where his ideas come from. They simply materialize out of a story concept or idea.

Chris Van Allsburg's art background is evident in his illustrations. Richness and texture are unique to his drawings. His design elements add depth and a sense of completion to the concept of a story. As a result, Mr. Van Allsburg has won many awards. His books have captured the imaginations of children everywhere.

Suggestions for Using the Unit Activities

Use some or all of the following suggestions to introduce students to *The Polar Express* and to extend their appreciation of the book through activities that cross the curriculum.

The suggestions are in the following sections:

- **Before the Book** includes suggestions for preparing the classroom environment and the students for the literature to be read.

- **Into the Book** has activities that focus on the book's content, characters, and themes.

- **After the Book** extends the reader's enjoyment of the book.

Before the Book

1. **Preparation:** Before you begin the unit, prepare the vocabulary cards, story questions, and sentence strips for the pocket chart activities. (See samples, patterns, and directions on pages 12–16).

2. **Themes:** Use *The Polar Express*, along with other stories and activities, to complete a unit on winter holiday customs. Explore such themes as "believe/make–believe," "the true spirit of Christmas," "modes of travel," "sound," and "the polar regions."

3. **Vocabulary:** Discuss the meanings of the following words before reading the story. Make several copies of the train pattern on page 14. Write one word on each train and display the trains on a pocket chart. (See page 12 for directions on making a pocket chart.)

polar	carols	thundered	sleigh
express	nougat	plains	reindeer
rustle	cocoa	barren	pranced
conductor	wolves	ocean lines	harnesses
outstretched	lean	North Pole	lurch
northward	flickered	Great Polar Ice Cap	imagine

4. **Background:** Set the stage for reading the book by asking the following questions and discussing students' responses.

- Have you ever taken a train ride?
- Has anything ever happened to you that you could not explain?
- What do you think of when you hear the word "mysterious"?
- What do you think of when you hear the word "magical"?
- What do you know about the polar regions (or the North and South Poles)?
- What is the true spirit of Christmas? Is it receiving presents?
- What is the difference between real and make-believe?

Suggestions for Using the Unit Activities *(cont.)*

Before the Book *(cont.)*

5. **Geography:** Ask whether anyone knows where the North Pole is and locate it on a globe. You may wish to explain or review the concept of directions on maps and globes and discuss why it is much colder at the North Pole than at other places on our Earth and why the days and nights are sometimes very long and sometimes very short. Explain that the book does not tell us where the boy lives.

6. **Using the Cover:** Display the cover of *The Polar Express.* Have children look for clues that might convey what the story will be about. Ask where they think the train might be going (refer to the word *polar* in the title). Ask the children which direction the train would be traveling if it is, in fact, going to a polar region (north/northward or south/southward).

7. **Personal Application:** Ask the students to imagine what they would do if they woke up late at night on Christmas Eve and saw a train standing in front of their house or apartment building. Ask them to listen as the story is read to discover where the train is going, who is on the train, and what will happen to them once they reach their destination.

   Suggestion: Before you read the book, attach ribbons to small jingle bells and hide one in each child's desk. After the story, tell children to look for a surprise in their desks. Ask if they can hear the bells ringing. Save the bells and use them for the science activity on sound (page 40).

Into the Book

1. **Story Questions:** Develop critical thinking skills with the story questions on page 15. The questions are based on Bloom's Taxonomy and are provided for each of Bloom's levels of learning. Reproduce several copies of the bell-shaped task card pattern on page 14 and write a story question on each bell. (See pages 13–15 also.)

2. **Vocabulary:** Review the vocabulary words on page 6.

3. **Story Summary Sentence Strips:** Cut out and laminate the sentences on page 16 to use on a pocket chart. Complete some or all of the following activities.

   • On the pocket chart, sequence the sentences in the order in which the events happen in the story.

   • Use the sentences to retell the story.

   • Divide the class into small groups and distribute a few sentence strips to each group. Ask the groups to act out the part of the story to which the sentences refer. In addition to these activities, you may wish to reproduce page 16 and have the students read the sentences aloud to a partner and/or take them home to read to a parent, caretaker, or older sibling.

4. **Story Scenes:** Students construct a scene from *The Polar Express* and write about some of the events in the story. Directions, patterns, and sentence blocks are provided on pages 20–21.

Suggestions for Using the Unit Activities *(cont.)*

Into the Book *(cont.)*

5. **Stick Puppets and Puppet Theaters:** Prepare the stick puppet theaters following the suggestions and directions on page 18. Allow the students to construct puppets by coloring and cutting out the puppet patterns on page 19 and gluing them to craft sticks or tongue depressors. Follow the suggestions at the bottom of page 18 for using the stick puppets. As an extension, give each student a piece of white construction paper to design a background scene from the story. Then, tell the children to arrange and glue down the puppet figures without sticks. The students can add speech bubbles and write something for each character to say.

6. **Polar Express Scrapbook:** Ask children to imagine they were on the Polar Express trip to the North Pole. Tell them they are going to make a scrapbook of their trip. Cut 4" x 6" (10 cm x 15 cm) colored construction paper rectangles for the front and back covers. Let students work alone or in pairs to write sentences about the scrapbook "photos" on pages 22–23. Follow the directions on page 23 to complete the remaining pages of the scrapbook.

   Direct children to design covers, staple the booklets together, and read them to a friend and/or grownup. **Note:** With younger or more inexperienced writers, compose the sentences together as a class, write them on the chalkboard, and let students copy them onto the booklet pages.

7. **Simile Stars:** Introduce children to similes (a figure of speech likening one thing to another by the use of "like" or "as"). Complete the similes on page 26. Use this as a whole-class activity or let more able children work alone or in pairs. Be sure to "share and compare" student responses.

   Suggestion: Children could draw pictures on white construction paper (perhaps of the train traveling toward the North Pole) and add their stars to the sky of their pictures.

8. **ABC Harness Bells:** As a whole class or in small groups, brainstorm a list of everything the boy saw on his trip to the North Pole. Give each student a 3" x 24" (8 cm x 61 cm) of brown construction paper and a set of bell patterns (page 24). Instruct students to choose eight of the words they wrote in their lists, write them on the bells, cut them out, arrange them in alphabetical order, and glue them to the construction paper (which serves as a harness). Display the harness bells.

9. **Bells Are Ringing!:** Take children through the entire writing process as they prewrite, revise, edit, and copy their final drafts onto the bell pattern on page 28. (If needed, make more than one copy for each student.) You may wish to initiate the writing with the following sentences: We read *The Polar Express* by Chris Van Allsburg. If I had met Santa, I would have asked him for . . .

   Display completed work on a bulletin board along with the harness bells in activity 8 above.

Suggestions for Using the Unit Activities *(cont.)*

Into the Book *(cont.)*

10. **"Found Poetry":** Follow the directions on page 27 to write a class "found poem." This is a creative and unique form of poetry. **Suggestion:** Include the class "found poem" in the Reader's Theater presentation. By doing so, several more children can have speaking parts.

11. **Finish the Picture:** Children follow directions on page 29 to complete the picture of Santa Claus delivering presents.

12. **Class Holly Wreath:** Encourage children to think about the "true spirit" of Christmas (giving instead of receiving, being with family, caring about others, love, friendship, etc.). After a class discussion, let each child complete a holly leaf (page 30). Attach leaves to a piece of colored tagboard to form a wreath. Add a large red bow and display in the room.

   Suggestion: You may wish to use this activity in conjunction with the Reader's Theater script, "The Spirit of Christmas," on pages 45–47.

13. **Rhyming Word Families:** Make a rhyming word train, using the pocket chart pattern on page 14 for the engine. Cut colored construction paper rectangles (with black circles for the wheels) to make the train cars. Have students work as a whole class to construct the rhyming word family trains. As an alternative, let groups of children each construct a train. When trains are completed, have the students "read" their trains. Other suggestions for the trains include days of the week, months of the year, contractions, and antonym, synonym, or homonym pairs.

After the Book

1. **Candy Houses:** Follow the directions on page 32 carefully. Be sure to ask in plenty of time for parent volunteers, donations of candy and other ingredients, and the loan of two heavy-duty table (not portable) mixers. Have students conclude this activity with candy house stories. Ask students to think about how they made their candy houses. Suggest introductory statements such as: I know how to make a candy house, this is how to make a candy house, what I loved about making candy houses, and we made candy houses.

Suggestions for Using the Unit Activities *(cont.)*

After the Book *(cont.)*

2. **The Polar Regions Game:** This game is a social studies activity and can be found on pages 35–39. Students will enjoy playing the game, and while doing so, they will be reinforcing what they have learned about these regions of the Earth. Following class reading and learning about the polar regions, construct class copies of the game. (Teacher information, which will help students to answer the game questions, is provided on pages 33–34.)

   To prepare the game, reproduce pages 35–39. You may wish to have students color the game boards. For greater durability, laminate these pages or glue them to heavy paper. Cut out the task cards. Separate the answer key on page 35 by cutting along the dashed line. (Players use the answer key to check their opponents' responses.) Store each game in a large envelope or resealable plastic bag.

3. **Ways to Travel:** As a class, brainstorm all the ways we can travel. Let each child choose a way to travel and write a short story about why he or she likes that way or would like to travel that way someday. Encourage students to use details to make their stories interesting. More advanced writers could trade and read each other's stories and list two or three unanswered questions on a piece of scratch paper. Then, have the authors edit their work by answering the questions as part of their story revisions. To display the stories, have each child draw a picture of his or her mode of transportation. Add the story to the inside of the picture.

4. **Ring Those Bells:** In this activity on page 40, children use real jingle bells to make predictions and discoveries about sound.

   Ask students to make predictions for each of these questions:

   • What will happen when you hold a bell by the top and shake it?

   • What will happen when you clutch the bell in your hand and shake it?

   Give each child a small jingle bell. Ask students to try each activity above. Encourage students to explain what they think happened. Then have students follow the directions on page 40 to complete this science activity.

Suggestions for Using the Unit Activities *(cont.)*

After the Book *(cont.)*

5. **Favorite Winter Pastimes:** This is a graphing activity and can be found on page 41. Talk about indoor and outdoor winter activities and then ask students to choose one favorite pastime from the four listed on a class chart. (Explain to students that although they may never have tried building a snowman or sledding down a hill, they can choose an activity they would like to try someday.) After completing the class graph, students fill out their individual graphs. (**Note:** As a whole class, individually, or in pairs, have students write two math problems using the data on the graph).

6. **Culminating Activities:** Celebrate the literature unit and the season with a day of enjoyment for students, teachers, and parents. Use the following activities and ideas for your culminating celebration.

   a. **Reader's Theater:** Have the students present the Reader's Theater program, "The Spirit of Christmas" (pages 45–47). Send the student-made invitation (page 48) to other classes, teachers, and parents. Suggestions for implementing a Reader's Theater format are provided on page 44.

   b. **Poetry:** Reproduce the poem "The Silver Bell" (page 17). Divide the children who do not have speaking parts in the script into four groups and assign each group a verse of the poem. Have the groups choral read and draw pictures of their verses. The groups of students can recite their verses at the close of the Reader's Theater presentation. For additional poems, refer to any number of available children's anthologies of poetry.

   Suggestion: Have the class compose a found poem (page 27) and include it in the program.

   c. **Music:** Reproduce "The First Gift of Christmas" on page 42. Practice the music and lyrics with the class. Have the class sing the song following the poetry reading. You may also wish to include "Jingle Bells" or other holiday favorites.

   d. **Ornaments:** Let students design and construct ornaments (page 25) to use on the tree needed for the production. **Note:** You can use a real tree, an artificial tree, or simply paint a tree (using green tempera) on a large piece of white butcher paper.

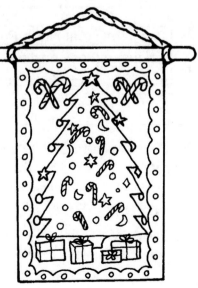

   e. **Holiday Banners:** Carefully follow the directions on page 43 to construct banners. You will be amazed at how beautifully these will turn out and how much parents will appreciate them. Display them around the room on the day of the program or have them gift wrapped and let students present them to their parents during the refreshment time.

   f. **Christmas Recipes:** Use the recipes on page 31 to prepare hot chocolate, Christmas cookies, and Christmas Popsicles to serve at the close of the program.

Pocket Chart Activities

Prepare a pocket chart for storing and using the vocabulary cards, the story question cards, and the sentence strips.

How to Make a Pocket Chart

If a commercial pocket chart is unavailable, you can make a pocket chart if you have access to a laminator. Begin by laminating a 24" x 36" (60 cm x 90 cm) piece of colored tagboard. Run about 20" (50 cm) of additional plastic. To make nine pockets, cut the clear plastic into nine equal strips. Space the strips equally down the 36" (90 cm) length of the tagboard. Attach each strip with cellophane tape along the bottom and sides. This will hold sentence strips, word cards, etc., and can be displayed in a learning center or mounted on a chalk tray for use with a group. When your pocket chart is ready, use it to display the sentence strips, vocabulary words, and question cards. (See sample chart below.)

polar   lurch   sleigh   lean   express

On Christmas Eve, a young boy saw a train standing perfectly still in front of his house.   **I Knowledge**

The boy took the conductor's outstretched hand and climbed aboard.   **II Comprehension**

On the train, children sang carols, ate candies with nougat centers, and drank hot cocoa.   **III Application**

They arrived at North Pole City where Santa chose the boy to receive the first gift of Christmas.   **IV Analysis**

How to Use the Pocket Chart

1. On gray construction or index paper, reproduce the train pattern on page 14. Make vocabulary cards as directed on page 6. To familiarize the children with difficult words and their meanings, present the vocabulary cards before reading the pages on which the words appear. Help students understand the word meanings by providing context clues.

   The patterns can be used to make "Amazing Author," "Wonderful Worker," "Great Reader" and other appropriate awards or incentives.

Pocket Chart Activities *(cont.)*

2. Reproduce several copies of the bell pattern (page 14) on six different colors of construction paper. Use a different paper color to represent each of Bloom's Levels of Learning.

For example:

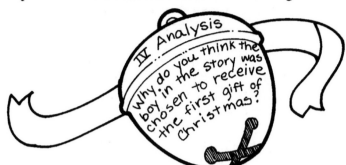

I.   Knowledge (green)

II. Comprehension (pink)

III. Application (lavender)

IV. Analysis (orange)

V.   Synthesis (blue)

VI. Evaluation (yellow)

Write a question from page 15 on the appropriate color-coded bell. Write the level of the question, the question, and the chapter section on the bell, as shown in the example above.

- Use the bell-shaped cards after the corresponding chapters have been read to provide opportunities for the children to develop and practice higher-level critical thinking skills. The cards can be used with some or all of the following activities.

- Use a specific color-coded set of cards to question students at a particular level of learning.

- Have a child choose a card, read it aloud, or give it to the teacher to read aloud. The child answers the questions or calls on a volunteer to answer it.

- Pair children. The teacher reads a question. Children take turns with their partners responding to the question.

- Play a game. Divide the class into teams. Ask for a response to a question written on one of the question cards. Teams score a point for each appropriate response. If question cards have been prepared for several different stories, mix up the cards and ask team members to respond by naming the story that relates to the question. Extra points can be awarded if a team member answers the question as well.

3. Use the sentence strips to practice oral reading and sequencing of the story events. Reproduce page 16. If possible, laminate the sentence strips for durability. Cut out the sentence strips or prepare sentences of your own to use with the pocket chart.

The boy asked for a silver bell from a reindeer's harness, but he lost it in Santa's sleigh.

The boy took the conductor's outstretched hand and climbed aboard.

Though the boy grew up, the bell still rang for him as it does for all who truly believe.

Pocket Chart Patterns

See pages 12–13 for directions.

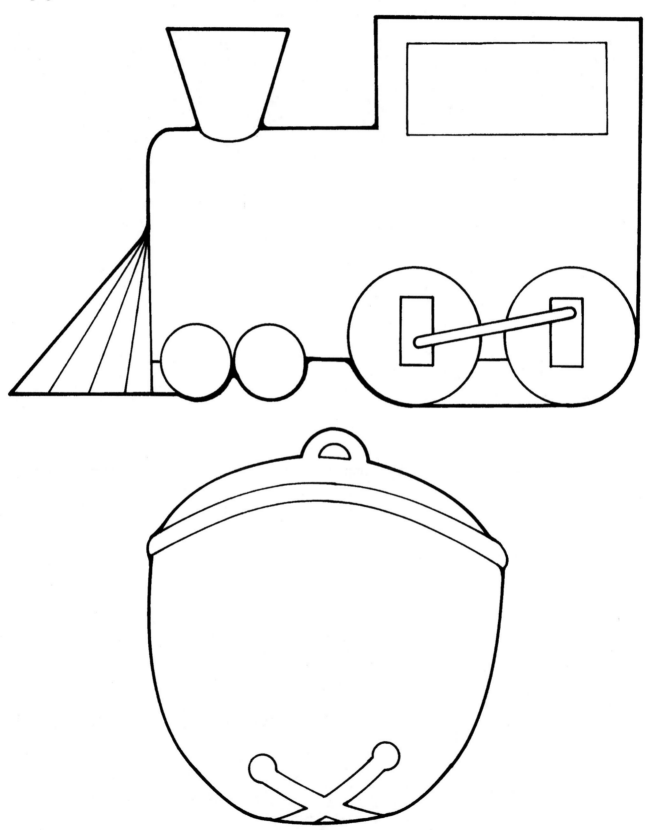

Story Questions

I. **Knowledge** (ability to recall learned information)

- Describe what the children did on the train.
- What is the Great Polar Ice Cap? How did the author describe it?
- What were some of the things the children saw on their trip to the North Pole?
- Who is telling the story? How do we know?

II. **Comprehension** (basic understanding of information)

- How do we know the train had to travel a long distance to reach the North Pole?
- Explain what is meant by a train "rolling over peaks and through valleys like a roller coaster."
- How did the other children react when the boy discovered he had lost the bell? What did they do?
- What do you think the conductor's job is? (Describe all the things you think he has to do on a trip).

III. **Application** (ability to do something with information)

- If a train had pulled up in front of your house, would you have been afraid to get on? Why or why not?
- If you had been able to stay for a day or two in North Pole City, what would you have wanted to do?
- If you had been selected by Santa to receive the first gift of Christmas, what would you have chosen? Tell why.
- Why didn't the boy's parents hear the bell? Why did they think it was broken?

IV. **Analysis** (ability to examine the parts of a whole)

- If you have ever taken a trip on a train, compare your trip to the one in the story.
- Were you surprised by the description of North Pole City in the book? How was it different from your idea of Santa's home?
- The elves cheered wildly when they saw Santa. Why do you think they did that?
- Why do you think the boy in the story was chosen to receive the first gift of Christmas?
- Who do you think selected the children who got to go on this particular trip? Tell how you think they were chosen.

V. **Synthesis** (ability to bring together information to make something new)

- What do you think would have happened if the train had broken down and the children had had to remain in North Pole City for a day or two?
- How would this story have been different if the boy had wished for a ride in Santa's sleigh instead of a silver bell?
- Tell what you might have done to try to get the bell back if you had been the one to lose it.

VI. **Evaluation** (ability to form and defend an opinion)

- How do the pictures help tell the story?
- What was the best part of this story? Tell why.
- Are you like the boy in the story? Tell how.
- Do you think the boy was imagining his trip to North Pole City?
- What was magical about the story? What was mysterious?
- Would you recommend this story to a friend? To a grownup? Why or why not?

Story Summary Sentence Strips

See page 13 (activity 3) for directions. You may wish to enlarge the strips for use in a pocket chart.

On Christmas Eve, a young boy saw a train standing perfectly still in front of his house.
The boy took the conductor's outstretched hand and climbed aboard.
On the train, children sang carols, ate candies with nougat centers, and drank hot cocoa.
They traveled northward through cold forests and climbed mountains so high it seemed as if they would scrape the moon.
They arrived at North Pole City, where Santa chose the boy to receive the first gift of Christmas.
The boy asked for a silver bell from a reindeer's harness, but he lost it in Santa's sleigh.
The Polar Express took the boy home. On Christmas Day, he discovered a package from Santa. Inside was his silver bell.
Though the boy grew up, the bell still rang for him as it does for all who truly believe.

"The Silver Bell"

The Polar Express stood perfectly still;
The conductor called out, "All aboard!"
I climbed up the steps with no time to spare . . .
The train gave a lurch, and the engine roared.

The miles mysteriously melted away,
The train thundered on toward the north,
Past villages, forests, and mountains
On a great adventure we had set forth.

In North Pole City, we slowed to a crawl;
A magical mist chilled the evening air.
The hour was late, but we each knew
The enchantment of Christmas was there.

In the spirit of love and giving
A silver bell was mine to receive.
It would ring forever sweet and clear
For all those who could truly believe.

By
Susan Kilpatrick

Stick Puppet Theaters

Make a class set of puppet theaters (one for each child), or make one theater for every 2–4 children.

Materials: 22" x 28" (56 cm x 71 cm) pieces of colored poster board (enough for each student or group of students); markers, crayons, or paints; scissors or craft knife

Directions:

1. Fold the poster board about 8" (20 cm) in from each of the shorter sides.

2. Cut a "window" in the center of the theater, large enough to accommodate two or three puppets. (See illustration.)

3. Let the children personalize and decorate their own theaters.

4. Laminate the theaters to make them more durable. You may wish to send the theaters home at the end of the year or save them to use year after year.

Suggestions for Using the Puppets and Puppet Theaters:

• Prepare the stick puppets, using the directions on page 8. Use the puppets and the puppet theaters with the Reader's Theater script on pages 45–47. (Let small groups of students take turns reading the parts and using the stick puppets.)

• Let children experiment with the puppets by telling the story in their own words.

• Read quotations from the book or make statements about the characters and ask students to hold up the stick puppets represented by the quotes or statements.

Stick Puppet Patterns

Story Scenes

Directions:

1. Give each student a large sheet of white construction paper or butcher paper.

2. Have students draw a scene from *The Polar Express*, as shown in the illustration to the right. You may wish to draw the scene on the chalkboard and have your students copy it.

3. Reproduce the stick figure puppets on page 19 to color, cut out, and glue to the pictures.

4. Reproduce and hand out a copy of the "Sentence Blocks" (page 21) to each student. Help students use the listed words in sentences that relate the words to the story. If age appropriate, reinforce the use of capitals, periods, quotations, commas in a series, contractions, possessives, etc.

5. Have students cut out and glue the sentence blocks to their pictures. It is not necessary to place the sentence blocks in a specific order.

A set of sentence blocks might look like this:

1. City The city was filled with factories where every toy was made.	**2. Train** The train slowed to a crawl and stopped.
3. Conductor The conductor shouted, "All aboard!"	**4. Santa** Santa asked me, "What would you like for Christmas?"
5. Elf The elf cut a bell from a reindeer's harness.	**6. Boy** The boy wanted one silver bell from Santa's sleigh.

Story Scenes *(cont.)*

Directions: Use with the "Story Scenes" activity on page 20.

1. City	**2. Train**
3. Conductor	**4. Santa**
5. Elf	**6. Boy**

Polar Express Scrapbook

Pretend you were on the Polar Express with the boy in the story. Make a scrapbook of your trip to the North Pole.

Directions:

1. Write a sentence or two describing each picture. (You can use the back of each page if you need more room.)

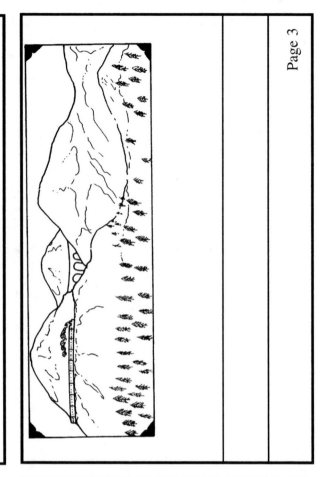

Page 1

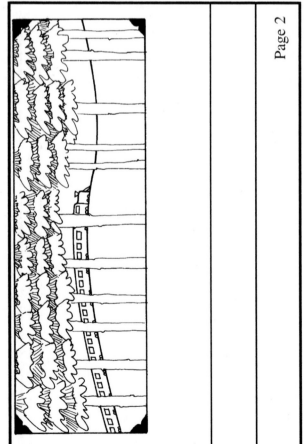

Page 2

Page 3

Polar Express Scrapbook *(cont.)*

Directions *(cont.)*:

2. In the picture frames on the bottom two pages, draw pictures that show what happened after you met Santa. Write about your pictures on the lines.

3. Make a cover: My Trip on the Polar Express by_____. Staple the scrapbook together. Read your scrapbook story to a friend!

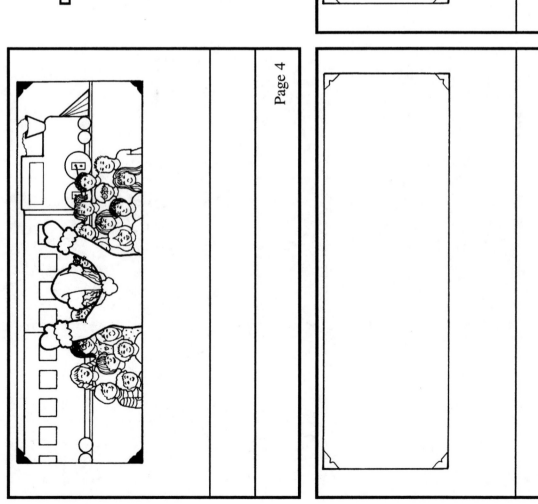

Page 4

Page 5

Page 6

ABC Harness Bells

See page 8 for teacher directions.

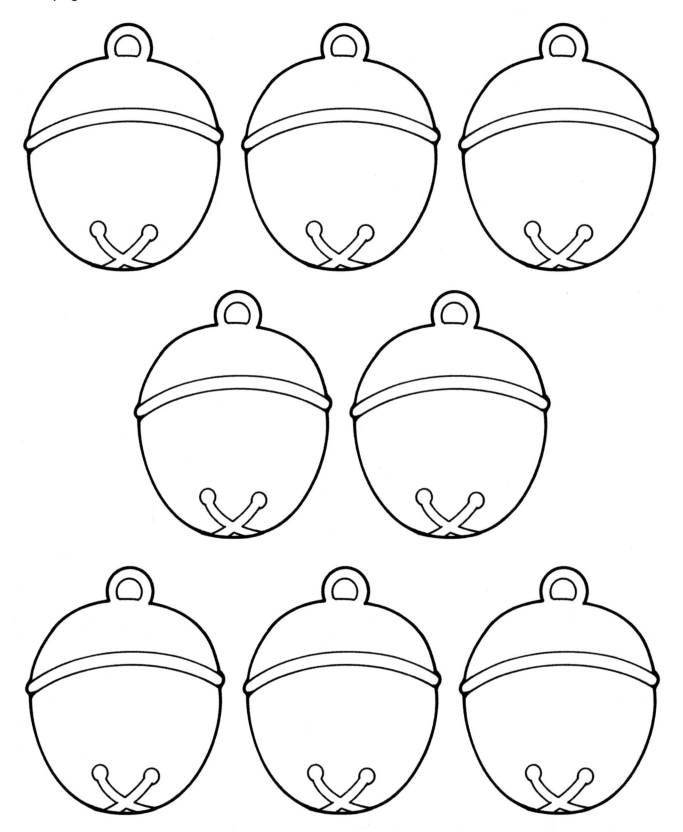

Holiday Ornaments

1. Color each ornament.
2. Attach a yarn loop through the hole.

3. Cut along the outside of this pattern. Fold on dashed lines. Tape or glue a yarn loop to the top.

Simile Stars

A *simile* is a figure of speech likening one thing to another by the use of "like" or "as." The author of *The Polar Express* used two similes in his story:

> **"The candies had nougat centers as white as snow."**

> **"We drank hot cocoa as thick and rich as melted chocolate bars."**

Work alone or with a partner to complete the "Simile Stars" below.

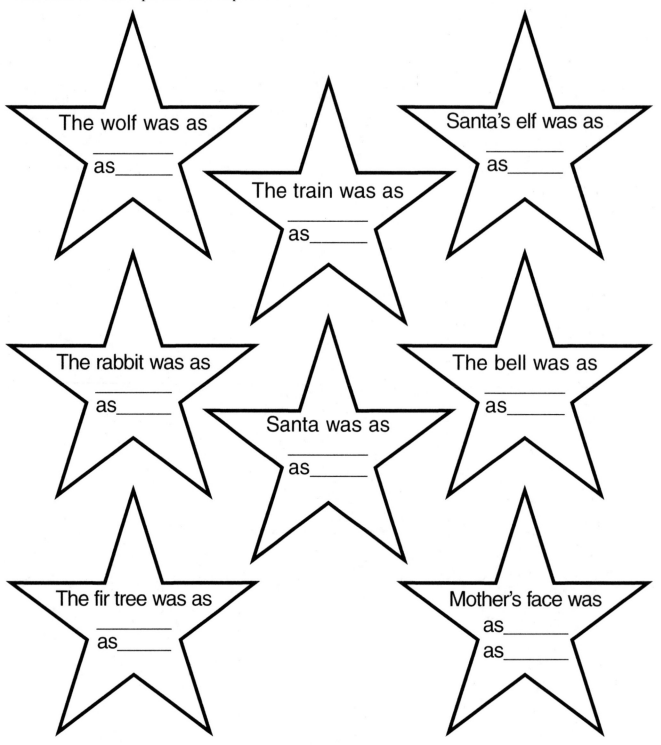

"Found Poetry"

A "found poem" is a collection of special words or phrases chosen from a piece of literature by groups of students. When read or spoken aloud, these selected lines form a "found poem," centering on the feeling or imagery created by the text. This activity enables students to return to the text and focus on vivid imagery, memorable passages, and exciting vocabulary.

The following lesson is a variation on the creation of the original "found poem."

1. Divide the book into six parts (sections). For each section, write a paragraph of dialogue or text that seems to capture the story line. Prepare "text cards" of the paragraphs. (These cards will be distributed to student groups.)

2. Glue each paragraph section to color-coded construction paper (one color for each section) and label the six parts (group 1 through group 6). Laminate the cards for durability.

3. Divide the class into small groups of four or five students. Distribute the text cards. (All the members of group 1 receive a copy of the group 1 text card, group 2 members receive the group 2 text card, etc.)

4. Instruct students to appoint a recorder. Children in each group select 4–8 special words or phrases from the text cards (not sentences) and list their choices on a piece of paper. Every member of the group should make at least one contribution to the list. (It may be necessary to model this activity using another piece of literature.)

5. The teacher then copies the words and phrases selected by the groups onto a chart for display. Children read and enjoy their new "found poem."

Suggestion: Duplicate the poem so that all the children can have a copy to take home.

"The Polar Express Poem"

Hissing steam
Squeaking metal
Train standing perfectly still
Apron of steam
Snowflakes fell
"All aboard,"
The Polar Express.
Other children
Pajamas and nightgowns
Christmas carols
Candy with nougat centers
Hot cocoa
Lights of towns and villages.
Cold, dark forests
Lean wolves
White-tailed rabbits
Quiet wilderness
Mountains so high
Scrape the moon.
North Pole
Huge city
Filled with factories
Christmas toys
Hundreds of elves
Santa's helpers.
Santa's sleigh
Reindeer
Pranced and paced
Silver sleigh bells
Magical sound
Elves cheered.
Any gift
Santa's giant bag
One silver bell
Gave a hug
Cut a bell
Reindeer's harness
The first gift of Christmas.

Use the sample poem and directions to guide students as they create a class "found poem." Display the poem on a chart and make copies for the children to take home.

Bells Are Ringing!

The boy in *The Polar Express* asked for one silver bell when Santa offered him anything he would like to have. On the bells below, write a story. Make sure you answer these questions in your story: What would you have asked for? What is your favorite part about the book? Did you or didn't you like the ending of the story? Remember to use details as you write.

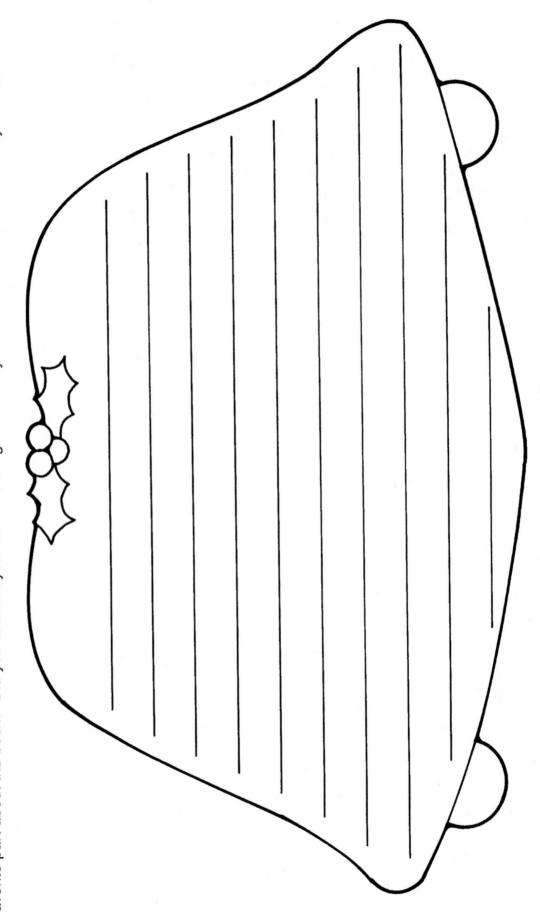

Finish the Picture

Follow the directions below to finish the picture on this page.

☐ 1. Color Santa's suit red and his belt and boots black.

☐ 2. Draw a wreath on the door. Color the door yellow.

☐ 3. Draw seven ornaments on the tree. Color two of them orange, one
       purple, two red, one yellow, and one blue.

☐ 4. Draw a yellow star on top of the tree.

☐ 5. Draw four presents under the tree.

☐ 6. Put a fire in the fireplace.

☐ 7. Draw a candy cane in Santa's hand.

☐ 8. Draw another candle on top of the mantle.

☐ 9. Color the rest of the picture.

☐ 10. Circle the words that describe Santa:

jolly	young	old	generous	short
thin	tall	mean	kind	bearded

Class Holly Wreath

Holiday Recipes

You may wish to serve the following foods after the Reader's Theater presentation.

Hot Chocolate and Sugar Cookies

Follow the package directions to make hot chocolate. Drop in one or two marshmallows before serving!

Prepare sugar cookies as suggested in the package directions. Let children decorate sugar cookies with the following frosting recipe:

Fluffy Butter Frosting

Ingredients:

- ¹/₃ cup (85 mL) soft butter or margarine
- ¹/₄ tsp. (1.25 mL) salt
- 1 tsp. (5 mL) vanilla
- 1 lb. (about 3¹/₂ cups/450 g) sifted confectioner's sugar
- about ¹/₄ cup (60 mL) milk

Directions:

This recipe makes 1¹/₂ cups (375 mL) of frosting. (You may need to double or triple this recipe.)

Divide the frosting evenly into three bowls. Make red, green, and blue frosting by adding a food coloring to each bowl.

Christmas Popsicles

Children will enjoy making and eating this delicious and healthy holiday treat.

Ingredients:

- 1 quart (1.1 L) yogurt
- 1 large can frozen cranberry juice
- 1 tablespoon (15 mL) vanilla
- ¹/₄ cup (60 mL) honey

Equipment:

- small paper cups or craft molds (one per student)
- craft sticks (one per student)
- large spoon and bowl

Directions:

Let the children take turns mixing the yogurt and juice together. When thoroughly mixed, add the vanilla and honey. Mix the ingredients again. Fill the paper cups half full and place a craft stick in the center of each cup. Freeze the Popsicle until it is hard. To eat, tear the cup away from the Popsicle.

As an extension, use tagboard to write sentence strips that provide the recipe directions. (Suggested sentence strips: Mix the yogurt and cranberry juice together. Stir the mixture until it is completely mixed. Add the vanilla and honey. Mix the ingredients again. Pour the mixture into cups. Put the craft sticks in the centers of the cups. Freeze the craft stick.) Cut up the sentences and let the children place the sentences in the correct order in a pocket chart.

Candy House

The delight on children's faces will be enough to make this a favorite class holiday activity for years to come.

Making the Frosting

Ingredients:

- 6 egg whites
- ⅓ cup (85 mL) water
- 1 box powdered sugar
- 1 tsp. (5 mL) cream of tartar

Procedure: Use a heavy table mixer (not a portable hand mixer). Remind children not to taste the raw egg whites. Beat all ingredients until thick. The mixture should stand up in peaks. Spread the frosting over the house and base and decorate the structure with candies, colored cereal, and candy sprinkles (used on cakes and cookies). This recipe covers about six houses.

Making the House and Base

Materials:

- tagboard
- glue
- stapler
- heavy cardboard
- small individual milk cartons (Have children save the small individual milk cartons they get in the school cafeteria.)

Procedure: Wash and dry the milk carton. Staple it closed. Cut a "roof" out of tagboard (about 2½" x 4"/6 cm x 10 cm). Glue and/or staple the "roof" onto the milk carton. Glue the "house" onto a heavy cardboard or clipboard base about 8" square (20 cm x 20 cm).

Tips:

- Put names on the bottoms of the bases before you begin.
- Ask a volunteer parent to pre-bag candy so each child has a variety in his/her own bag. (Suggested candies to use include: Lifesavers, Red Hots, M&M's, Skittles, gumdrops, small slices of red licorice, candy canes, and red and green sprinkles.)
- Have a packet of papers/tasks ready for the children to work on while they are waiting for their houses to be frosted: word searches, crosswords, simple art projects, etc.
- Instruct the children not to put heavy pieces of candy on the roof because they will slide off.
- Ask two or three volunteer parents to help mix the frosting and frost the houses. Have two mixers available if possible. You will need to make five or six batches of frosting for a class of 32 children. Use plenty of frosting on each house.

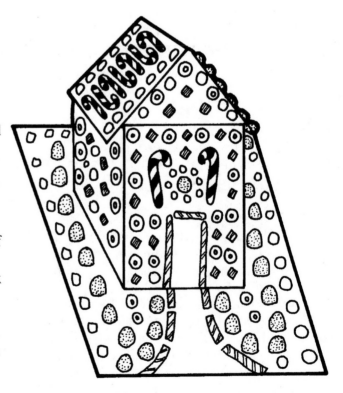

Life in the Polar Regions

The North Polar Region

At the north pole lies a frozen sea called the Arctic Ocean. Near this polar ice cap, in the Arctic Circle, are the cold northern areas of Alaska, Canada, Greenland, and Siberia, which are home to the "Inuit" people, or Eskimos. The word "Inuit" means "real people," while "Eskimo" is an Indian word meaning "eater of raw meat."

The Eskimos, a warm, gentle people, live in small groups in the cold, harsh northern land sometimes called "the top of the world." Winter temperatures often stay 25 degrees below zero for weeks at a time. The vast, treeless plains, or "tundras," are covered with snow, and the water is frozen much of the year. However, in summer the snow and ice melt for a short time, and some plants and grasses can be seen growing on the tundras.

Eskimo villages have homes made of wood and whalebone and are covered with seal skins and earth. Igloos, which are made of carefully cut blocks of snow, are used only as temporary shelters during hunting trips. Seal oil is burned for warmth and light.

The Eskimos hunt for land and sea animals, such as walrus, seal, polar bear, caribou, wild reindeer, birds, and fish, to use for food. The Eskimos' clothing must be very warm to protect them from the severe cold. They wear parkas, boots, and mittens made from the hides and furs of the animals they hunt.

Because it is necessary to follow the herds of animals, travel is important to the Eskimo. Two types of boats are used. The "kayak" is a one-man canoe and the "umiak" is a large boat that can hold an entire family. Snowshoes are used to travel short distances on land. Sleds pulled by dogs called "huskies" are still sometimes used to travel great distances across the snow. The most famous dog sled race, the Iditarod, is more than 1,000 miles (1609 km) long. It begins in Anchorage, Alaska, and ends in Nome, and can take up to one month to finish.

Life in the Polar Regions *(cont.)*

The North Polar Region *(cont.)*

Eskimo life is becoming much more modern. Today many Eskimos buy their food and clothing at stores, use oil and electricity, and travel by snowmobile, car, and motorboat.

The South Polar Region

Antarctica, the fifth largest continent, is found at the southern tip of the world. Much of the south polar region is permanently covered in a thick shield of ice and is the coldest and windiest place on Earth. During the summer months (May to July at the north pole and November to January at the south pole) the sun shines even at midnight. In winter, the sun does not rise, and the poles are almost continually dark.

There are no cities in Antarctica. Only scientists and explorers brave this region as they carry out experiments and study the environment. The polar winter is too cold for most animals, but a few hardy species survive there. Penguins, covered by a layer of fat and feathers, are well adapted to the snow and icy waters where they catch krill, fish, shrimp, and squid to eat. Penguins can swim 15–20 miles (32 km) an hour.

Once a year, large groups of penguins gather on land in nesting areas called rookeries. The baby penguins, or chicks, are hatched after two months, and are cared for by both the mother and father penguins. They must protect their young from enemies such as seagulls, skuas, and seals.

The largest kind of penguin, the Emperor penguin, stands over three feet (90 cm) tall and weighs up to 90 pounds (41 kg).

Scientists have found that protecting the polar regions is important to the future well-being of the entire Earth, and measures are being taken to preserve the poles and prevent them from being foolishly exploited.

For more information, see books listed in the bibliography on page 48.

The Polar Regions Game

To play the Polar Regions Game you will need the game board (pages 38–39), game markers (pennies, buttons, paper squares, etc.), task cards (pages 36–37), and a die or spinner.

Directions: This game is for two to three players or two teams of two players. (Teams act as one player, but they can answer the questions together.) Each player will need a game marker.

1. Place the task cards face down in a pile near the game board.

2. Take a task card and answer the question.

3. If you answer correctly, roll the die or spin the spinner and move the number of spaces shown.

4. If you answer incorrectly, stay on the same space.

5. The first player or team to reach the end wins.

- -

Answers for The Polar Regions Game

1. The north polar region or the far north or the top of the world

2. Antarctica or the south polar region

3. Antarctica

4. polar bear, seal, walrus, caribou

5. dogsled and boat

6. a rookery

7. fat and feathers

8. krill, fish, shrimp, squid

9. 15–20 miles (24–32 km) an hour

10. burn it for heat and light

11. when they are hunting on the tundra

12. large, flat land where the Eskimos hunt

13. from the store

14. parkas, boots, mittens

15. a dogsled race

16. Anchorage to Nome

17. Canada, Greenland, Siberia, U.S.A.

18. "real people"

19. food, clothing, and other products

20. a canoe

21. one

22. a boat

23. a whole family

24. a kind of dog used by Eskimos to pull sleds

25. a barren desert of ice

26. a chick

27. 2 months

28. the Emperor penguin

29. seagulls, skuas, seals

30. birds

The Polar Regions Game *(cont.)*

④ Name at least two animals important to the Eskimo.	③ What continent is found at the bottom of the world?
⑧ What do penguins eat? (Name two things.)	⑦ What do penguins have that keep them warm? (Name two things.)
⑫ What is the tundra?	⑪ When do Eskimos stay in igloos?
⑯ Where does the Iditarod begin and end?	⑮ What is the Iditarod?

② Where do penguins live?	① Where do Eskimos live?
⑥ What is the penguins' nesting area called?	⑤ Name two ways Eskimos travel.
⑩ What do Eskimos do with seal oil?	⑨ How fast can penguins swim?
⑭ What do Eskimos wear to keep warm?	⑬ Where do Eskimos get some of the supplies they need?

The Polar Regions Game *(cont.)*

17 Name at least two of the four countries where Eskimos live.	**18** The Inuit people are called Eskimos. What does "Inuit" mean?	**19** For what do Eskimos use the animals they kill?	**20** What is a kayak?
21 How many people can ride in a kayak?	**22** What is an umiak?	**23** How many people can ride in an umiak?	**24** What is a husky?
25 What is the great polar ice cap?	**26** What is a baby penguin called?	**27** How long does it take for a baby penguin to hatch?	**28** What is the name of the largest kind of penguin?
29 Name at least one enemy of penguins.	**30** What kind of animals are penguins?		

Game

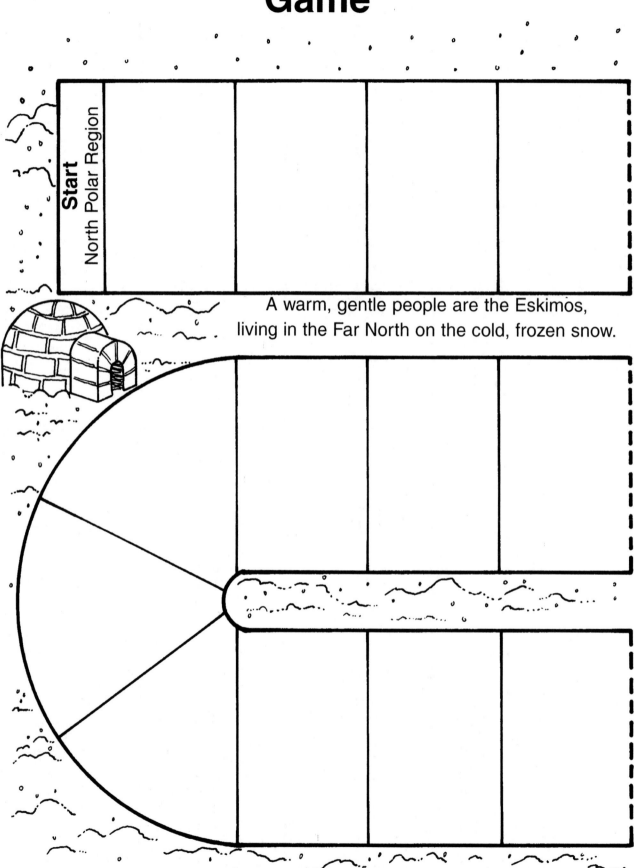

Start

North Polar Region

A warm, gentle people are the Eskimos,
living in the Far North on the cold, frozen snow.

38

Board

Down in Antarctica near the South Pole,
the penguin lives in the icy cold.

Finish
South Polar Region

Ring Those Bells

There are many kinds of sounds, but all sounds are the same in one way. They are all made by things moving back and forth very fast, or vibrating.

Directions: Read each sentence box on the right. Match the information in each sentence box with its picture. Write the sentence box number in the picture box. Then, cut apart the four picture boxes. Glue them in the spaces on the right in the correct order.

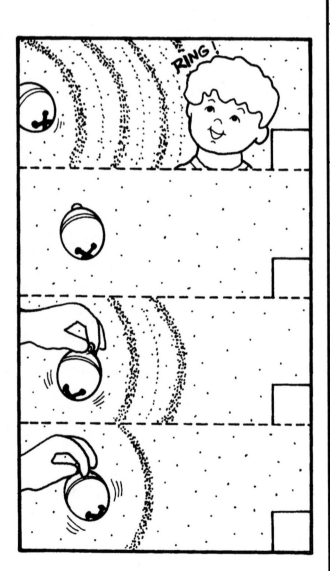

① The air is made up of molecules (invisible, tiny bits or particles).

② When a bell rings, the clapper hits the bell. The bell moves back and forth very fast (or vibrates).

③ The vibrating bell bumps into air molecules, which bump into other air molecules, which bump into other air molecules.

④ The sound travels in waves until some of the air molecules bump against your ear and you hear the bell.

My Favorite Winter Pastime

20				
19				
18				
17				
16				
15				
14				
13				
12				
11				
10				
9				
8				
7				
6				
5				
4				
3				
2				
1				
0	Read a book by the fireplace	Build a snowman	Drink hot chocolate and eat popcorn	Go down a hill on a sled

After completing the class graph above, use the data to write at least two sentences. Use the back of this page. (Work alone or with a partner.)

"The First Gift of Christmas"

©1995 Words and music by Mary Ellen Hicks (used by permission)

1. The   first gift of Christ-mas is —   what I want to give. It's —
2.   first gift of Christ-mas —   is a   mys-te-ry that's true.— One might
3.   first gift of Christ-mas —   is be- liev-ing you are blessed. —

all that I will ask for, it's — how I want to live. I can't touch or   ev-er
search and ne-ver find it — while it's ve-ry clear to you. I don't know why some can't
Faith makes ma-gic hap-pen —when you put it to the test. You don't have to be a

taste it, yet I know when it is there. The first gift   of   Christ-mas is—   one that I will
see that if you dream and if you dare, The first gift   of   Christ-mas is—wait-ing for them
child — to en-joy this gift so rare. The first gift   of   Christ-mas can be-long to those who

share.   2. The   there. With eyes to see won-ders that hap-pen each day, our hands reach to

help and to   hold.   Our ears ring with mu-sic from   kind words we say. This

gift is more   pre-cious than gold.   3. The   care.

Holiday Banners

Here is a great gift idea for children to make and parents to treasure!

Materials:

- inexpensive white or off-white fabric
- coarse sandpaper — one sheet 8½" x 11" (22 cm x 28 cm) for each child
- paper towels
- crayons
- scratch paper
- pencils
- marking pens (permanent)
- dowel sticks — one per child about 13" (33 cm) long
- colored yarn
- iron
- pinking shears (optional)
- tissue paper (for wrapping gift)

Preparation:

- Cut fabric into approximately 10" x 14" (25 cm x 36 cm) rectangles (one for each child).
- Use pinking shears for an interesting edge, which also prevents raveling of the material.
- Talk with students about possible subjects for their banners: a Christmas tree, a wreath, an elf, Santa, a snowman, an angel, etc.

Procedure:

1. Have children use pencils to design banners on scratch paper. When they are satisfied with their pictures, have children use crayons to sketch their designs on the sandpaper. Encourage them to include some kind of border and to fill up the space provided (very tiny details will not show up). Be sure to leave a 2" (5 cm) blank space along the top. This will be folded over the dowel stick. Do not write words on the sandpaper. They will come out backwards!

   A.

2. When the picture is completed, lay the sandpaper face up on a pad of newspapers. Lay the fabric over the sandpaper and cover the fabric with two layers of paper toweling to protect your iron. (See illustration A.)

3. Iron the area slowly for several seconds.

4. Check to see if the color has come through on the fabric. Peel the fabric away from the sandpaper.

5. Optional: Let children write "Merry Christmas" or "Happy Holidays" on their banners with marking pen. Teacher may write child's name and the date in a bottom corner. (See illustration B.)

6. Use a hot-glue gun to attach the banner to the dowel.

7. Tie colored yarn on each end as shown.

8. Roll the banner up and wrap it with tissue paper.

B.

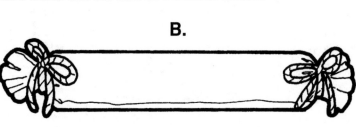

Reader's Theater

Reader's Theater is an exciting and easy method of providing students with the opportunity to perform a play while minimizing the use of props, sets, costumes, or memorization. Students read the dialogue of the announcer, narrators, and characters from prepared scripts. The dialogue may be verbatim from the book, or an elaboration may be written by the performing students. Sound effects and dramatic voices can make these much like radio plays.

In a Reader's Theater production, everyone in the class can be involved in some way. The 12 speaking parts in this Reader's Theater, in addition to the poem on page 17 and the song on page 42, maximize student involvement. Encourage class members to participate in off-stage activities as well, such as greeting the audience and assisting behind the scenes.

It is not necessary to wear costumes for a Reader's Theater production, but the students can wear signs around their necks indicating their speaking parts. Prepare signs by writing the reader's character on a piece of construction paper or tagboard. Laminate it, if possible, for durability. Then, staple a necklace-length piece of yarn to the top of the paper (or punch holes and tie with yarn).

Prepare script booklets for the readers as well. It is well worth the time, and you will have them to use again and again. You will need one script booklet for each reader, including the announcer, the narrators, and the teacher. Highlight (with yellow marking pen) all lines spoken by an individual reader. Write the title and author of the piece being read and the name of the character being highlighted on the outside cover of the booklet. It is a good idea to include the poem and the song in the script booklets. Glue (do not staple) the pages of the script into the booklet and laminate them for durability. Use a long-arm stapler to complete the script booklets. (**Note**: You will need song sheets for each of the singers and poem sheets for the readers of the poem.)

For a 2–3 page script, construct the booklet as follows:

For a 3–6 page script, construct the booklet as follows:

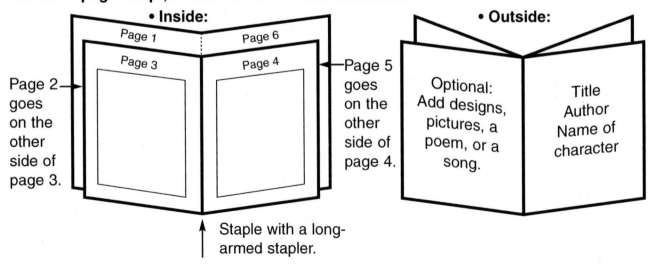

The Spirit of Christmas

(A Reader's Theater written by Susan Kilpatrick)

(**Note:** At the front of the room, there should be either a real or an artificial tree. Or, paint a tree on a piece of white butcher paper and hang it up in front of the room. Children should have paper ornaments they have made ready to hang on the tree.)

Announcer: Welcome to our Reader's Theater presentation of "The Spirit of Christmas." Our readers are as follows:

Announcer:	**Narrator 4:**	**Doctor:**
Narrator 1:	**Mayor:**	**Boy:**
Narrator 2:	**Store Owner:**	**Girl:**
Narrator 3:	**Bank President:**	**Young Child:**

Narrator 1:   Our story takes place in an ordinary town somewhere in the U.S.A.

Narrator 2:   The mayor of the town is in charge of the annual tree decorating ceremony.

Narrator 3:   The townspeople have started to gather in the town square. They have brought decorations to hang on the tree.

Narrator 4:   Shh-hh! Here comes the mayor. The ceremony is about to start.

Mayor: Welcome to our annual tree decorating ceremony. As each of you comes forward to place a decoration on the tree, I invite you to say a few words about the true spirit of Christmas.

Narrator 1:   The first person to come forward is the owner of a large department store in the town.

Store Owner: *[Hangs an ornament on the tree.]* I think the true spirit of Christmas is shopping, and I hope all of you will come down to my store to buy gifts for everyone you know. After all, presents are what Christmas is all about, and I have the best bargains in town.

Mayor: Thank you very much. Who would like to be next?

Narrator 2:   The president of the bank is the next person to come forward.

Bank President: *[Hangs an ornament on the tree.]* The true spirit of Christmas can be found in all the beautiful decorations, and I want to invite all of you to visit my home. You won't believe the gorgeous decorations in my house. I have angels, candles, holly, Santas . . . and you must see the huge wreath on my door.

The Spirit of Christmas *(cont.)*

Mayor: Thank you for that generous invitation. Who else has an ornament for our tree?

Narrator 3: The next person to step up is a doctor at the local hospital.

Doctor: *[Hangs an ornament on the tree.]* I'm sure our bank president's home is quite lovely inside, but you really must drive by my home to see the decorations in my yard and on my roof. We have thousands of blinking lights and a 10-foot wooden sleigh pulled by eight reindeer. Now that's what Christmas is really about!

Mayor: Yes, yes. I've seen your display, and it is unbelievable. Who's next?

Narrator 4: Two children walk quickly up to the mayor.

Boy: *[Hangs ornament]* I like the presents and the decorations, but I think the true spirit of Christmas is all the great food there is to eat . . . turkey and stuffing and mashed potatoes . . . or maybe tamales . . . and, best of all, the desserts! I'm getting hungry just standing here!

Girl: *[Hangs ornament]* I like the food, too, but I agree with the store owner that the presents are the best part—the more the better! This year, I'm getting a talking doll *and* a new bike.

Mayor: Thank you, children. Well, our tree is looking quite beautiful. This is a town that certainly knows how to celebrate Christmas.

Narrator 1: Just then a young child came forward.

Young Child: Excuse me, Mr. Mayor, but what about *people?* You've only talked about *things.*

Mayor: People? I'm not sure I understand what you're talking about.

Young Child: Well, aren't *people* more important than *things* like decorations and presents and fancy food? No one has even mentioned family and friends.

Mayor: Hmmm. I wonder if we're missing something. Let's ask and see if anyone else has an idea. Raise your hand if you would like to share what *you* think is the true spirit of Christmas with the rest of us.

[Mayor calls on several people sitting in the "audience" who then share their ideas about the true meaning of Christmas. This could be planned out ahead of time or completely spontaneous.]

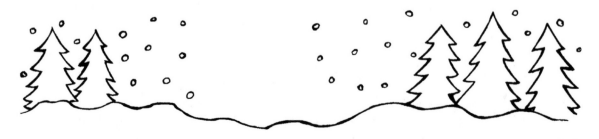

The Spirit of Christmas *(cont.)*

Mayor: Thank you for those wonderful ideas. You've given us a lot to think about.

Store Owner: I'm going to start spending more time with my family.

Bank President: I'm going to see what I can do to help people who don't have as much as I do.

Doctor: I know a lot of sick people who would be glad to have some visitors.

Boy: We could take them some presents and some food. I've heard that it's better to *give* than to receive anyway.

Girl: We could sing some Christmas carols and try to cheer people up. We all know some wonderful songs.

Young Child: Now this is more like it! Can we get started right away?

Mayor: Yes! That's a great idea. Everyone meet in half an hour at city hall.

Narrator 2: The whole town changed that night. They stopped thinking only about themselves and their own presents and decorations.

Narrator 3: They began to treat others more kindly and spent time making other people happy.

Narrator 4: They thought about other people all year long, not just at Christmas time. They discovered that as *they* did this, they became happier people, too!

Announcer: We hope you enjoyed our presentation of "The Spirit of Christmas." We will now recite a poem called "The Silver Bell" by Susan Kilpatrick. Our readers for the poem are _____ and _____ .

[Note: See poem on page 17. As they read, children could display pictures that depict scenes from The Polar Express. *The verses of the poem could be attached to the backs of the pictures.]*

Announcer: Our class will now sing a song called "The First Gift of Christmas" by Mary Ellen Hicks.

[Note: See song on page 42.]

Announcer: This is the end of our program. Thank you for being such good listeners.

[Note: If the class has composed a "found poem," page 27, several children could read it aloud as part of this program.]

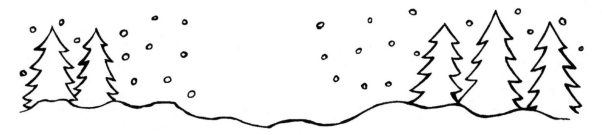

Bibliography

Other books by Chris Van Allsburg

The Garden of Abdul Gasazi. (Houghton Mifflin, 1979)
Jumanji. (Houghton Mifflin, 1981)
The Wreck of the Zephyr. (Houghton Mifflin, 1983)
Just a Dream. (Houghton Mifflin, 1990)
The Mysteries of Harris Burdick. (Houghton Mifflin, 1984)

Related Literature

Bonners, Susan. *A Penguin Year. (*Delacorte, 1981)

Brett, Jan. *The Wild Christmas Reindeer. (*Putnam Pub. Group, 1990)

Byles, Monica. *Life in the Polar Lands (Animals, People, Plants). (*Scholastic Inc., 1993)

Cowcher, Helen. *Antarctica. (*Soundprints, 1990)

Gill, Shelley. *Kiana's Iditarod. (*Paws Four Pub., 1984)

Joose, Barbara M. *Mama, Do You Love Me?* (Chronicle Books, 1991)

Kendall, Russ. *Eskimo Boy (Life in an Inupiaq Eskimo Village). (*Scholastic Inc., 1992)

Khanduri, Kamini. *Polar Wildlife.* (EDC, 1993)

Prelutsky, Jack. *It's Christmas* (poetry). (Greenwillow, 1991)

Seuss, Dr. *How the Grinch Stole Christmas. (*Random Books Young Read, 1957)

Stone, Lynn M. *Antarctica. (*Childrens, 1985)

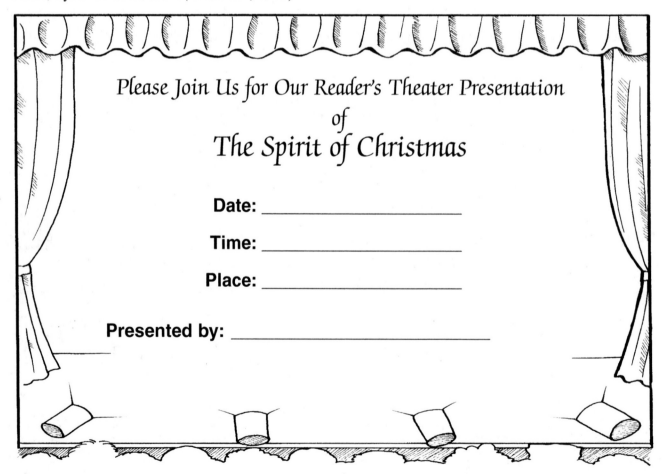

Please Join Us for Our Reader's Theater Presentation
of
The Spirit of Christmas

Date: _____

Time: _____

Place: _____

Presented by: _____